Swimming a...
Diving

A description of all aspects of
swimming and diving; from le...
the strokes to Olympic highbo...
diving, and from swimming th...
English Channel to the fast, ex...
game of water polo. There are p...
of tips for beginners, and many
photographs of the great names...

InterSport

Swimming and Diving

Tony Duffy

**Colour photographs by
Tony Duffy**
All-Sport Limited

Wayland/Silver Burdett

InterSport

The world of international sport seen through the cameras of some of the world's greatest sports photographers, showing in action both children and the stars they admire.

Basketball	On Horseback
Cycling	Snow Sports
Golf	Soccer
Gymnastics	Swimming and Diving
Ice Sports	Tennis
Motorcycling	Track and Field

Frontispiece **A Great All-Rounder** – Tracey Caulkins of the U.S.A., one of the finest individual medley swimmers in the world.

First published in 1981 by Wayland Publishers Limited
49 Lansdowne Place, Hove, East Sussex BN3 1HF, England
© Copyright 1981 Wayland Publishers Limited
ISBN 0 85340 796 7

Published in the United States by Silver Burdett Company, Morristown, New Jersey
1981 Printing
ISBN 0 382 06515 8

Phototypeset by Trident Graphics Limited, Reigate, Surrey
Printed in Italy by G. Canale & C.S.p.A., Turin

Swimming and Diving

A description of all aspects of swimming and diving; from learning the strokes to Olympic highboard diving, and from swimming the English Channel to the fast, exciting game of water polo. There are plenty of tips for beginners, and many colour photographs of the great names.

Contents

Introduction   6
How to get started   8
Breaststroke   13
Freestyle   19
Backstroke   24
Butterfly   30
Individual medley   37
Training and competition   41
Long-distance swimming   44
Diving   51
Synchronized swimming   56
Water polo   60

Index   64

Introduction

It seems likely that man has always been able to swim. Certainly, in the days of ancient Greece and Rome, swimming was an important part of a warrior's training. In Japan in the Middle Ages, the Emperor made it compulsory for swimming to be taught in schools. Legends of the Pacific islands feature their heroes swimming or surfing.

There are not many sporting skills that can save your life, but swimming is one of them. Each year, many children lose their lives through drowning. Learning to swim is, therefore, a very sensible decision to make.

The competitive side of swimming is very important. In terms of prestige and importance, it ranks second only to track and field in the Olympic Games. It has its own championships at World, Pan-American, Commonwealth and National levels.

In no other sport are the champions so young. Swimmers have won Olympic and World Championships at fourteen years of age and under. The average age of most national teams is sixteen, and many champions have retired by the age of twenty.

Gold for Gould – Another medal for Shane Gould of Australia, who has held all freestyle world records during her career.

Bright Young Star – Julia Bogdanova of the U.S.S.R. was a world champion at the age of twelve. In the 1980 Moscow Olympics she took the bronze medal in the 200 m breaststroke, and Russian girls also won gold and silver.

Four main swimming strokes are now widely practised. These are freestyle (or front crawl), breaststroke, backstroke and butterfly. A fifth one, side stroke, although it was the standard racing style in the early days of competition, is not used competitively today, and it is seldom taught to beginners. We shall look at these four main strokes in the following chapters.

How to get started

Most children's introduction to swimming is during family holidays on the coast, or through school swimming lessons.

Most swimming pools have qualified teachers who, for a modest fee, will teach a child to swim. Proper instruction is a great advantage because a coach will teach the correct stroke technique. Many children teach themselves or learn from friends and, unfortunately, pick up bad stroke techniques which are very difficult to change later. So try to get it right at the beginning.

The one thing that will help you to learn quickly is to relax in the water. A relaxed body will float and be supported by the water. Remember also that you can breathe out under the water. Your greatest obstacle in learning to swim may be your fear of the water, but once you overcome this, and it won't take very long, you'll be surprised at how quickly you improve.

Once you have learned to swim you may want to compete against other children. There is a marvellous system of competitions for all ages at school, district, and national

A Good Start – A group of children in California, U.S.A., get some expert coaching on how to begin a race. It is very important to learn the correct techniques right at the start, since bad ones are difficult to change later.

level. If you find you have an aptitude for swimming it makes sense to join your local swimming club. Here you will be coached and you can train with other children of your own standard. You will also compete for your club against other clubs and you will make many friends. There is a good social side to most swimming clubs.

These clubs are inexpensive to join. If you don't know where your nearest club is, contact your local council offices or city hall.

Otherwise contact the Amateur Swimming Association at *Harold Fern House, Derby Square, Loughborough, Leics. LE11 0AZ*.

In America, children should contact the U.S. Olympic Committee at *1760 Boulder Street, Colorado Springs, Colorado 80909*.

Your sports teacher at school will advise you about the proficiency badges which you can obtain as you progress up the ladder of swimming. The A.S.A. have a campaign called 'every boy and girl a swimmer' and, wherever you live, your national swimming association is just as interested in helping you in any way they can, so don't hesitate to write to them for advice.

The age group programme is a marvellous system of competition designed to encourage those who show promise. It is possible to get into the national junior and senior teams, and to compete in international age group championships through this scheme. If you have the will, there is certainly a way!

Tomorrow's Champion? – The look of determination suggests that this youngster certainly hopes to be.

10

Breaststroke

This is the slowest of the four strokes but, in most cases, it is the safest. Usually a swimmer can keep going longer on this stroke than on any other. It is also suited to most water conditions. The swimmer has the advantage of seeing exactly where he is going because he is facing forwards.

The leg movement in this stroke is very similar to that of a frog when it is swimming – kicking out and away and then together again. The arms are moved forward and then pulled to the side. The head bobs up and down with each stroke, to take in a gulp of air when it is up, and breathe it out under water when it is down. The art is to synchronize the arm and leg movements correctly and, as in all swimming strokes, to be relaxed and confident in the water.

This is one stroke at which Britons have always been successful. The 1976 Olympic Champion was David Wilkie, and one of the best breaststrokers in the world at the moment is Duncan Goodhew, the 1980 Olympic Champion. Both of these swimmers attended American universities, and their

Coming Up for Air – Julia Bogdanova fills her lungs before plunging forward again.

On the Crest of the Wave – Britain's Duncan Goodhew, 100 m gold medallist in the 1980 Olympics. Duncan's long, fluent stroke helps him to travel very smoothly through the water.

swimming has benefited from the regular high-class competition and the excellent facilities for training common to most American colleges.

As you will see from the picture, Duncan is bald, and you might notice that this is not unusual among champion swimmers. The reason swimmers shave their heads is to make them faster through the water. Sharks, dolphins and other fish don't have any hair because water flowing through the hair would cause a drag effect, slowing down progress. Swimmers also shave their arms, legs and chests for the same reason, but not all have the courage to shave their heads, even for the sake of saving an extra tenth of a second in a race. In Duncan's case, a rare childhood illness resulted in him losing his body hair, so the decision was made for him.

In women's swimming, Anita Lonsborough was Britain's last breaststroke gold medallist, at the Rome Olympics in 1960. The event is now dominated by three Russian girls who, between them, hold all the records.The most famous is Julia Bogdanova, who was a champion at the age of twelve.

Championship races in a 50-metre pool will involve one turn in the 100 metres and three turns in the 200 metres. The turning technique is very important and vital time can be saved by a good turn. The swimmer must touch with both hands and then swivel round and kick off from the wall.

Turning Point – Anita Lonsborough demonstrates the breaststroke turn. The swimmer must touch with both hands before swivelling round and pushing away from the wall. *(above)*

Blowing Bubbles – David Wilkie breathes out under water as his arms begin their long pull backwards. *(right)*

Freestyle

The front crawl, commonly known as free-style, is the fastest and most popular stroke. The swimmer turns his head to the side to breathe in, and breathes out under the water, synchronizing these movements with a forward entry of the arms, one after another, and a deep pull back under the body. At the same time, the legs kick up and down alternately, performing what is known as a 'flutter kick'.

Some champions prefer a fast leg kick, with as many as six or eight beats of the legs to one complete arm stroke. Others just use the legs as a sort of rudder, moving them in time with the arm strokes. There is no right or wrong way. It depends on the method which suits you best and which happens to be most fashionable with the coaches at the time. In competition, freestyle races are held at the following distances: 100 metres, 200 metres, 400 metres, 800 metres (for women only) and 1500 metres (for men only). There are also relay races for men at 400 metres and 800 metres, and at 400 metres for women.

Strong-arm Tactics – Irina Aksyonova of the U.S.S.R. speeds through the water, surrounded by spray.

Hanging Loose! – This picture illustrates the arm recovery technique used by freestylers. The hand is not held rigid since this would increase water resistance.

There have been some great freestyle champions: Duke Kahanomoku, the Hawaiian surfer who trained in the Pacific rollers off his native island; Johnny Weissmuller, the American who later became the most famous 'Tarzan' in films; Mike Wenden, the Australian who had a dreadful style but great speed; and Mark Spitz of the U.S.A., the most famous champion in the history of swimming, who won seven gold medals at the Munich Olympics. This is still a record for any sport. Britain's greatest freestyler

Take a Deep Breath – Cornelia Ender breathes in before launching herself into the pool. Swimmers try to dive in at as shallow an angle as possible so that they can get into their stroke quickly.

was Bobby McGregor of Scotland, who came second in the 100 metres at the Tokyo Olympics. He might well have won the gold medal if he had made a good start.

On the women's side, America and Australia have produced the greatest champions at freestyle. The most famous are Dawn Fraser of Australia, who won three consecutive Olympic 100 metres titles; Donna de Verona of the U.S.A., who won three gold medals in Tokyo; Debbie Meyer who, at sixteen, won three golds at the 1968 Olympics;

Out on Her Own – Barbara Krause of East Germany, who won the 100 m and 200 m freestyle events in the Moscow Olympics, and broke her own 100 m world record twice in the process. *(above)*

Shane Gould of Australia, who has held all the freestyle records at one time or another; and Cornelia Ender, the blonde East German who won four golds and one silver at the Montreal Olympics.

All major races are now timed electronically with the aid of touch-pads at the end of the pool. These pads calculate the time to a thousandth of a second when the swimmer touches at the end of a race. This degree of accuracy is especially important in 100-metre races where all eight competitors may finish within one second of each other.

A Watchful Eye . . . on the other competitors. Shane Gould sizes up her chances of winning. *(right)*

22

Backstroke

As the name implies, you swim this stroke on your back. Your arms rotate alternately, windmill fashion, going into the water behind your head and pulling through to the side. The legs are kicked up and down as in freestyle, to create forward movement. There is no breathing problem on this stroke.

Most great backstrokers tend to have long, thin bodies and large hands and feet. In fact, big hands and feet are a great advantage to the swimmer in any stroke, as they can scoop the water better. In a boat, if you have a paddle with a large blade you will obviously go faster than if you have one with a small blade, and it is the same principle with the hands and feet in swimming.

The main problem in backstroke is the fact that you cannot see where you are going. Therefore, it is not a suitable stroke for recreational swimming or long distance swimming. In backstroke races there is a line of flags above the water, 10 metres from each end of the pool, so that the swimmers know when they are approaching the wall.

Perhaps the greatest backstroker of all

At Full Stretch – Swimmers hurl themselves away from the wall at the start of a backstroke race.

25

In Flight – John Naber, perhaps the greatest backstroke swimmer of all time, leaps clear of the water to get a fast start.

Almost There – Zoltan Verraszto of Hungary just failed to win a gold medal in Moscow; he came second in the 200 m backstroke and third in the 400 m individual medley. *(above)*

time was the giant American, John Naber. He dominated the swimming events in the Montreal Olympics, winning both backstroke gold medals and putting an end to the reign of that other great champion, East Germany's Roland Matthes, who had won four golds at the previous two Olympic Games.

America's Linda Jezek is the current women's World Champion, having taken over from another great East German swimmer, Ulricha Richter.

Making a Splash – Kiki Caron of France, swimming high in the water. *(right)*

Butterfly

This is the most recently developed of all the strokes, having been brought out in 1935 as a racing adaptation of breaststroke. It is also the second fastest after freestyle. It is an extremely tiring stroke, requiring a lot more strength than the other strokes. As a result, most butterfly swimmers have broad, powerful shoulders and big chests.

The style of the butterfly stroke is the closest man can get to the swimming motion of the dolphin. In fact, the double leg kick used in this stroke is called the 'dolphin leg kick'. The arms come over together and scoop back underwater. The legs perform a double kick which propels the swimmer forward for the next stroke. The body flips up and down in a series of undulating movements. It is an exciting stroke to watch when done well. As in breaststroke and backstroke, there are races at 100 metres and 200 metres.

The greatest butterfly swimmer of all time was Mark Spitz. His record, set at the 1972 Munich Olympics, stood for nearly eight years. This is an extraordinary length of time for a record to stand in swimming. In no

The Deposed Queen – East Germany's Andrea Pollack. Her world records have both been broken by Mary Meager. *(above)*

Water Wings – Avis Willington shows why it's called the 'butterfly' stroke. *(right)*

30

Victory Roar? – Mike Bruner, 200 m butterfly world record-holder, pushes himself on to the finish. Like most butterfly swimmers, he has very strong shoulder muscles.

other sport is the rate of improvement so rapid. Olympic records set by men twelve years ago are now being beaten by fourteen- and fifteen-year-old girls.

This rapid improvement in times is mainly due to increased training, both in and out of the water. Training out of the water is known as 'land conditioning', and sometimes accounts for one third of a swimmer's total training time. It is often done on multi-purpose weight-training machines, on which the swimmer can simulate the various stroke

The Fastest Flyer – Mary Meagher of the U.S.A., holder of both butterfly world records. Because of the American boycott of the Moscow Olympic Games, she was unable to compete against Pollack and her other rivals.

movements and practise them against increasingly heavy weights on the machine.

Americans have always dominated butterfly swimming, with great champions like Mike Bruner, another bald swimmer.

In women's competition, the big East German girl, Andrea Pollack, dominated the 1976 Olympics, winning her first title when she was fourteen. Since then, a new star has arisen, an American schoolgirl called Mary T. Meagher, who has broken both Pollack's world records.

SuperSpitz! – America's Mark Spitz, winner of seven gold medals at the Munich Olympics, and world record-holder for nearly eight years.

Individual medley

Silver for the Golden Girl – Sharron Davies of Great Britain swam the race of her life to take the silver medal in the 400 m individual medley in Moscow. *(above)*

Beaten in Her Absence – Tracey Caulkins of the U.S.A. was not able to prevent Petra Schneider of East Germany from winning the 400 m individual medley in world record time. She was another victim of the boycott. *(left)*

The best tests of a swimmer's all-round ability are the individual medley races at 200 metres and 400 metres respectively. In these events the swimmer starts on the butterfly, switches to backstroke, then breaststroke, and finishes on freestyle.

You cannot afford to have a weak stroke in this event and, as you may imagine, it is a really gruelling race. Just as a swimmer develops a rhythm on one stroke, he must change to the next.

One of the world's greatest individual medley swimmers is Jesse Vassallo, who was born in Puerto Rico but emigrated to the U.S.A. when he was a child. He trains with the famous coach Mark Schubert in California. He trains extremely hard and is known in swimming as the 'Iron Man'.

The greatest all-round female swimmer is Tracey Caulkins of the U.S.A. She won five gold medals at the 1978 World Championships in Berlin when she was fifteen years of age. Britain's best medley swimmer is Sharron Davies from Plymouth, who won both gold medals at the Commonwealth Games in

Edmonton, Canada. She is trained by her father, and is currently the 'Golden Girl' of British swimming.

Besides the individual medley, there is also a 400 m medley relay for teams of four, in which swimmers hand over to each other after each leg. The order of the strokes differs from that of the individual medley; the first member of the team swims backstroke, and then he hands over to the second swimmer for the breaststroke leg. The third swims butterfly, and the final leg is freestyle.

Looking at some of the photos, you might notice how sleek the girls' swimsuits are. In the old days they were made of wool and linen, but just as hair has a drag effect in water, so does fabric. To reduce this to a minimum, some swimsuit companies have spent thousands of pounds researching and testing new materials and new styles of suits to give maximum freedom of movement. The latest suits are made of Lycra and are incredibly light, weighing only two or three ounces when dry. The water does not cling to this material but runs off it. Obviously a bikini-type swimsuit would be even lighter and less restrictive but, under the existing rules, a girl's swimsuit must be one-piece.

Well Suited – Swimsuits like this one are the product of a great deal of costly research. They are specially designed to reduce 'drag' and increase the swimmer's speed.

The Iron Man – Jesse Vassallo is known for his tough training programme. *(left)*

Training and competition

In very few other sports is the training as intensive as it is in swimming. Many top swimmers have three training sessions each day; early morning, noon and late afternoon. During these sessions the swimmers drive themselves almost to exhaustion, and burn up so much energy that they must eat huge meals to replace it.

You will probably have noticed that the use of goggles is very common. This is to protect the swimmer's eyes from soreness caused by the presence of chlorine in the water. Chlorine is added to the water for sanitary purposes. If a swimmer spends four or five hours a day in the pool, his eyes would get very sore without goggles.

The time to do the heavy basic training is during the winter, when there are few competitions. In the summer you will want to reach your peak for the important competitions. Before these events your coach will ease down your training sessions (this is called 'tapering') and work on your speed and

Clocking In – Swimmers spend hours each day racing against the stop-watch in an attempt to take a split-second off their race-time.

technique to bring you to a fine pitch for your competition. You must learn to trust your coach's judgement and do what he says. If you work with him, instead of against him, you will stand a better chance of success.

The one thing the coach cannot give you is the will to win – the competitive spirit. It is often this which separates the winners from the 'also-rans'. The fortunate few who possess it will push themselves a little bit harder in a race. Without this will to win you will never get right to the top, so be prepared to be honest with yourself, and if you don't have it don't be ashamed. It's better to find a branch of the sport that you can enjoy, perhaps diving, synchronized swimming, water polo or long-distance swimming. Otherwise just swim for fun or at club level because, make no mistake, there is only hard work, pain and sacrifice ahead if you are set on being an Olympic champion.

Competition is also a test of character. Everyone gets nervous as race-time approaches. Some will succeed in hiding their nerves better than others, but all will be suffering from them to some degree. Learn to control your nerves, don't let them control you. Adopt a positive attitude and tell yourself that you've done all the hard work in training so you deserve victory. Tell yourself that you're as good as the other swimmers. Remind yourself how good you'll feel after the race is won and how bad you

Loosening Up – Cornelia Ender gets a warm-up massage before a training swim. It is vital to make sure that your muscles are supple before you force them to do a lot of hard work.

It was All Worthwhile! – The look of relief on Cornelia Ender's face speaks for itself. The training may have been gruelling but the reward was victory.

will feel afterwards if you know that you didn't give one hundred per cent. There is no disgrace in losing, if you do your very best.

Be sensible on the day of the race. Don't burn up energy unnecessarily. Leave yourself plenty of time to digest your last meal before the race. Seek your coach's advice on warming up before the race. Always wear your tracksuit or bathrobe until the starter calls you to your blocks, as a warm, loosened-up body is like a car engine that has been running for some time. It runs much more smoothly than one that has just been started.

Above all, whether you win or lose, try to be sporting about it. Be a modest winner and a gracious loser – a pat on the back for the winner doesn't take a lot of effort!

Long-distance swimming

Just over 100 years ago a British sea captain called Matthew Webb set out to swim the English Channel to France. The channel is 36 km (22 miles) across at its narrowest point, but the strong tides and currents sweep a swimmer miles off course, so he ends up by swimming much further.

There are many other hazards to this swim. The water is very cold, the waves are often very choppy and can spring up suddenly. There are shoals of stinging jellyfish and, in recent years, slicks of oil to contend with. To make things worse still, the English Channel is also one of the busiest sea routes in the world, with all kinds of shipping from huge oil tankers to cross-channel ferries.

For hour after hour the gallant captain struggled on despite the cold and the currents, and eventually, after twenty-two hours in the water he landed in France. He became a celebrity overnight. In those days it just wasn't considered possible. It was almost as if someone today set out to try to swim the Atlantic.

Since that first marvellous achievement,

On the Rocks – Mary Beth Colpo at the end of a swim from Catalina Island to the Californian coast. The waves can sweep a swimmer on to the rocky headland, causing painful cuts and bruises.

Best in the Long Run – Cynthia Nicholas has swum the English Channel faster than anyone else. This swim is very demanding because of the strong tides and currents, the cold, shoals of jellyfish and the busy shipping lanes which the swimmer encounters on the way.

channel swimming has become one of the greatest tests of endurance and courage open to a swimmer. Since Webb's day, swimmers have achieved double-crossings; that is a non-stop swim there and back. There have even been attempts at a three-way swim but this is probably asking too much of the human body.

The greatest channel swimmer of all time is a blonde Canadian girl of nineteen, Cynthia Nicholas. She has beaten the men's record by a number of hours. Some people claim that women are better suited to these long-distance endurance events because they have a greater percentage of body fat, which helps to keep them warm. Others believe that they have a greater tolerance to pain. Whatever the reason, this is one sport where women can beat the men in open competition.

Another great long-distance swim is from Catalina Island to the coast of California. Here the swimmer has two other problems to contend with. One is the occasional presence of sharks, and the swimmer sometimes uses a large wire-mesh cage dragged along by an accompanying boat to protect himself. The other is the rocky headland where they land, which can cause cuts and bruises if an exhausted swimmer is carried on to these rocks by the big waves. In this event too, the men take second place to a girl – Mary Beth Colpo, a Californian. In the photo you can

It's All Too Much – Cold and exhausted, Diana Nyad gives up her attempt to swim the Channel.

Early Morning Dip – Two swimmers set off at 5 a.m. in order to catch the outgoing tide. They have smeared lanolin grease on their bodies to give some protection from the cold.

see the cuts she sustained whilst trying to land on the rocks after her swim.

Even children of thirteen or fourteen are now attempting the channel swim. It is usually better to attempt the swim in relays, say eight swimmers from one school taking it in turns to swim a couple of miles each.

Diving

Diving is a thrilling sport which goes hand in hand with swimming. In Olympic competitions there are two types of contest, a 3-metre springboard event and a 10-metre platform event; the latter is known as highboard diving.

In each of these competitions, the diver must perform a set number of basic compulsory dives and certain other dives of his own choice. Each dive is marked by a panel of judges and the diver with the highest aggregate mark is the winner. To help those divers attempting the most difficult dives, each dive is allocated a 'degree of difficulty' figure. The average mark given by the judges is then multiplied by the 'degree of difficulty' figure to give a final score for each dive.

Springboard and highboard diving require very different skills. In the former, the diver must learn to control and use the 'whip' of the flexible springboard. The highboard, however, is a fixed platform with no spring in it at all, but the highboard diver is 7 metres higher up, so he doesn't really need any extra height in which to execute his

Free Fall – Jenny Chandler of the U.S.A. performs one of her diving routines.

51

Perfect Pike – Britain's Christopher Snode demonstrates the 'pike', one of the basic elements in diving.

spectacular mid-air routine.

These routines are very gymnastic. They basically comprise somersaults, twists and 'pikes'. A pike manoeuvre involves touching the toes with the legs straight. It is not uncommon for a diver to include a mixture of these elements in one dive. For example a double twisting one-and-a-half somersault requires the diver to leave the board and execute first two twists and then one-and-a-

The American Eagle – Greg Louganis swoops
down towards the water from the 10-m
highboard.

half somersaults before entering the water.

The entry is vitally important; the legs
must be straight and the feet together with
the toes nicely pointed. A diver can enter the
water feet first or head first, the latter being
the more common.

When diving from the highboard, you will
reach quite a speed by the time you hit the
water, and this can give you a serious jolt if
you don't make a correct entry. Most people

imagine that the diver's fingers are pointed but this is not so. If you watch closely you will see that the highboard divers link their hands at the thumbs and 'punch' a hole in the water for their heads to follow. A bad entry can result in a diver being knocked out, so when you are practising always make sure you have a friend or a coach standing by in case of accident.

Two of the greatest divers in the world today are Greg Louganis of the U.S.A. and Christopher Snode of Britain. They both have slim bodies which give them a clean 'line' in the air. This is just what the judges look for, since the essence of a good dive is making a difficult manoeuvre look graceful and easy.

Women's diving is also very graceful. The Olympic and World Champion on the springboard is another American, Jenny Chandler. She had the advantage of being able to use the 3-metre diving board in her parents' pool when she was young.

One of the greatest diving displays in the world is put on by the 'skydivers of Acapulco'. In this Mexican resort some brave local men plunge down from the cliff tops into a tidal gorge at a moment when it is empty of water. They have to time their take-off exactly right so that the waves are coming into the gorge as they start their dives. By the time they hit the water, it is deep enough to allow them safe entry.

Take That! – A diver prepares to literally punch a hole in the water.

Synchronized swimming

There are many girls who are good swimmers but, for one reason or another, don't succeed in competition. These girls need not give up the sport, as synchronized swimming is the perfect outlet for their talent and enthusiasm.

It is best described as water ballet. There are three types of competition; solo, pairs and team. The team consists of four to eight girls. The routines, which begin on the side of the pool, are performed to music. After the girls enter the water they effect graceful movements in time to the music, and many of these movements are performed under the water. For this reason, the best way to watch synchronized swimming is through the underwater observation windows that are built into some pools.

The judges look for grace, musical interpretation, degree of difficulty, and harmony. Make no mistake, it is not as easy as it may look. The best girls go through an entire programme without making one splash as they glide, dive and hover in the water. Very often they wear glittering

Synchronized Stars – The Santa Clara Aquamaids in one of their balletic displays. Their graceful precision won them the World Team Championship in 1975.

56

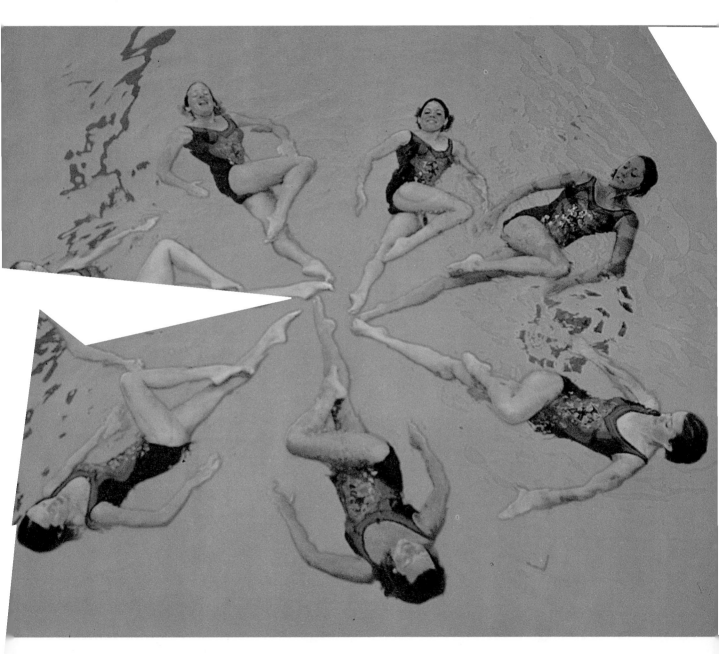

Winning Smiles – Helen Vanderburg and Michele Calkins, the 1978 World Champions. *(above)*

costumes and head-dresses to add to the visual impact of the programme.

The Santa Clara swimming club in America produces some of the best synchronized swimmers and, in 1975, they won the World Team Championship. But, at the 1978 World Championships in Berlin, the Canadians were dominant, with Helen Vanderburg winning both the solo and, with Michele Calkins, the pairs titles.

Winning Smiles – Helen Vanderburg and Michele Calkins, the 1978 World Champions. *(above)*

The Water Wheel – The best way to watch underwater routines like this is through observation windows built into the side of the pool. *(right)*

Water polo

Until recently the rough, tough game of water polo was played exclusively by boys. But there are now a number of girls' teams in America, Holland and Germany.

In order to play the game well, you need to be a fast swimmer over short distances, with plenty of stamina and, above all, the ability to handle a ball. The game is similar in principle to soccer, with two goals and goalkeepers, and the rudiments of the game are just as easy to understand. However, there are seven players in each team rather than eleven, and only their heads and arms are above the water. The referee has to be the busiest man in the game, as he keeps a sharp eye open for fouls below the surface, as well as concentrating on all the other aspects of play.

Apart from synchronized swimming and relay racing, water polo is the only real team event in swimming. Although the game began in Britain, the Russians, Yugoslavs and Hungarians have dominated the sport since the 1930s, but the Italians have recently emerged as a great team.

Pushing Forward – Water polo players can 'carry' the ball on the wave produced by their movement through the water. *(above)*

Rough and Tumble – A player sees his chance to gain possession from an opponent, and lets nothing get in his way! *(right)*

On Target – The top corners of the goal are two of the most difficult areas for the goalkeeper to defend, and this attacker has chosen her spot perfectly.

Index

Aksyonova, Irina   18

Bogdanova, Julia   7, 12, 16
Bruner, Mike   32, 33

Calkins, Michele   58
Caron, Kiki   29
Caulkins, Tracey   2, 36, 37
Chandler, Jenny   50, 54
Colpo, Mary Beth   45, 48

Davies, Sharron   37
de Verona, Donna   21

Ender, Cornelia   22, 42, 43

Fraser, Dawn   21

Goodhew, Duncan   13, 14–15, 16
Gould, Shane   6, 22, 23

Jezek, Linda   28

Kahanomoku, Duke   20
Krause, Barbara   22

Lonsborough, Anita   16
Louganis, Greg   53, 54

Matthes, Roland   28
McGregor, Bobby   21
Meagher, Mary T.   30, 33
Meyer, Debbie   21

Naber, John   26–7, 28
Nicholas, Cynthia   46–7, 28
Nyad, Diana   48

Pollack, Andrea   30, 33

Richter, Ulricha   28

Santa Clara Aquamaids   57, 58
Schneider, Petra   37
Snode, Christopher   52, 54
Spitz, Mark   20, 30, 34–5

Vanderburg, Helen   58
Vassallo, Jesse   37, 38
Verraszto, Zoltan   28

Webb, Matthew   44
Weismuller, Johnny   20
Wenden, Mike   20
Wilkie, David   13, 17
Willington, Avis   31